FAIR ISLE

Crochet Projects

LEISURE ARTS, INC. • Maumelle, Arkansas

Add excitement to your crochet with color. It's easier than you think, especially with this beginner's guide to Fair Isle technique. Get the basics on pages 4-5, and then you'll be on your way to make any of these beautiful designs. Choose from two hats, a cowl, a scarf, and two afghan & pillow sets. Have fun adding color to your décor or your wardrobe. Why should the knitters have all the fun?

FAIR ISLE TECHNIQUE 4

LAUREL LEAVES HAT & SCARF 6

HUGS & KISSES HAT & COWL 16

STARS & DIAMONDS AFGHAN & PILLOW 24

ZIGZAGS & DIAMONDS AFGHAN & PILLOW 34

GENERAL INSTRUCTIONS 44

YARN INFORMATION 47

MEET MELISSA LEAPMAN 48

Fair Isle Technique

Fair Isle is a technique used to create patterns with many colors. Only two colors are used on each row or round and the unused color is worked over, weaving it into the fabric.

GAUGE WHILE CHANGING COLORS

For stitches to look uniform *(Fig. 1)* and for the project to match the finished size given in the instructions, it is essential to maintain stitch gauge while changing colors. This will also ensure that you will have enough yarn to finish your project.

Fig. 1

CHANGING COLORS

Colors are changed as the last sc of a color section is made, working the last sc of the color you are using to within one step of completion and completing the sc with the next color.

To change colors in sc, insert your hook in the next sc, YO and pull up a loop (2 loops on hook); drop yarn to **wrong** side of work, with new color, YO and draw through both loops on hook *(Fig. 2a)*.

Fig. 2a

To join a new color with a slip st, insert the hook in the first st of the rnd. Pick up the color specified, YO with the new color and draw through the st and the loop on the hook *(Fig. 2b)* to complete the slip st.

Fig. 2b

This method allows the first chain for the next round to be in the new color *(Fig. 2c)*.

Fig. 2c

When working sc in the round, it's easy to prevent two skeins of yarn from being twisted when changing colors. Always keep the first color used on a round above the second color no matter which color you are changing to *(Fig. 2d)*.

Fig. 2d

YARN FLOATS

Yarn floats are created when a color is carried **loosely** on the **wrong** side of the work *(Fig. 3a)*.

Fig. 3a

Work over the floats on the next row or round *(Fig. 3b)*, enclosing them within the fabric to prevent the yarn from showing on the front or back.

Fig. 3b

HOW TO FOLLOW A CHART

The chart shows each sc as a square, indicating what color each sc should be.

To keep your place, a ruler, a piece of paper, or a sticky note can be placed **above** the row or round you are working. You need to see the row or round you have just completed to ensure you are working the correct color.

LAUREL LEAVES

HAT & SCARF

Laurel leaves crowned victors in ancient Rome and this set makes you a winner, too! Featuring attractive bands of alternating leaves, it is a snap to crochet before your next back-to-nature outing.

LAUREL LEAVES

HAT & SCARF ●●○○ EASY +

SHOPPING LIST

Yarn (Medium Weight) MEDIUM 4

[3 ounces, 197 yards

(85 grams, 180 meters) per skein]:

Hat

- ☐ Color A (Black) - 1 skein
- ☐ Color B (Ecru) - 1 skein
- ☐ Color C (Red) - 1 skein
- ☐ Color D (Grey) - 1 skein

Scarf

- ☐ Color A (Black) - 1 skein
- ☐ Color B (Ecru) - 1 skein
- ☐ Color C (Red) - 1 skein
- ☐ Color D (Grey) - 1 skein

Crochet Hook

- ☐ Size H (5 mm)

  or size needed for gauge

Additional Supplies

- ☐ Yarn needle (for Hat only)

GAUGE INFORMATION

In Fair Isle pattern,

15 sc and 15 rows/rnds = 4" (10 cm)

Gauge Swatch: 4" (10 cm) square

Ch 15; finish off.

Row 1 (Right side)**:** Working in back ridge of chs ***(Fig. 4, page 45)***, join yarn with sc in first ch ***(see Joining With Sc, page 45)***; sc in each ch across; finish off: 15 sc.

Rows 2-15: With **right** side facing and working in Back Loops Only ***(Fig. 5, page 45)***, join yarn with sc in first sc; sc in each sc across; finish off.

FINISHED SIZES
Hat: Finished circumference 19¼" (49 cm)
Scarf: 6" wide x 55½" long (15 cm x 141 cm)

STITCH GUIDE

FRONT POST DOUBLE CROCHET
(abbreviated FPdc)
YO, insert hook from **front** to **back** around post of st indicated ***(Fig. 7, page 46)***, YO and pull up a loop (3 loops on hook), (YO and draw through 2 loops on hook) twice.

BACK POST DOUBLE CROCHET
(abbreviated BPdc)
YO, insert hook from **back** to **front** around post of st indicated ***(Fig. 7, page 46)***, YO and pull up a loop (3 loops on hook), (YO and draw through 2 loops on hook) twice.

SINGLE CROCHET 2 TOGETHER
(abbreviated sc2tog)
Pull up a loop in each of next 2 sc, YO and draw through all 3 loops on hook **(counts as one sc)**.

HAT CHART

Write the color name of the yarn you're using in the Color Key.

COLOR KEY

- Color A ________
- Color B ________
- Color C ________
- Color D ________

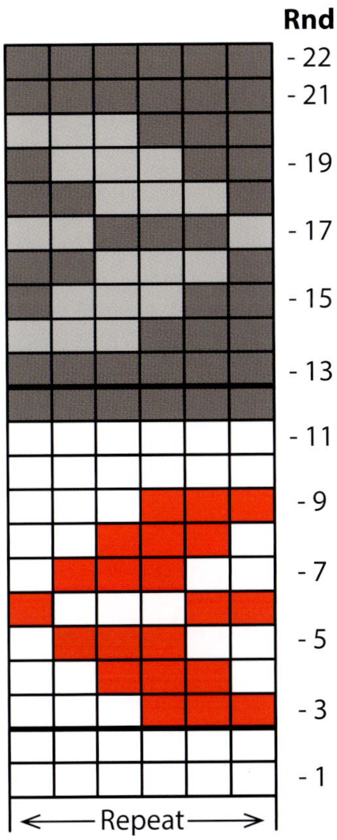

On all rounds, follow the Chart from **right** to **left.**

SCARF CHART

Write the color name of the yarn you're using in the Color Key.

COLOR KEY

- Color A ________
- Color B ________
- Color C ________
- Color D ________

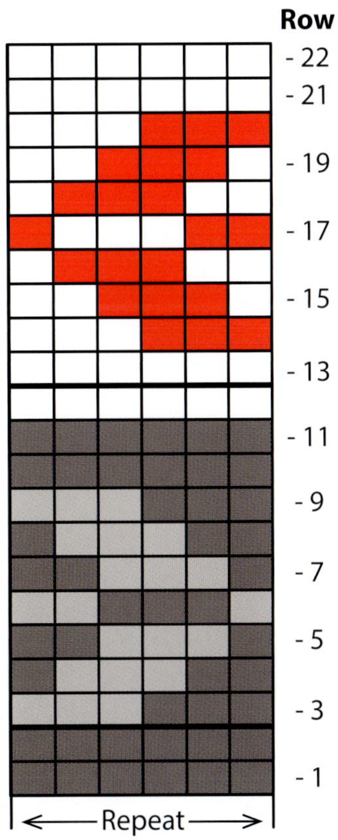

On all rows, follow the Chart from **right** to **left.**

HAT

RIBBING

With Color A, ch 72; being careful **not** to twist ch, join with slip st to back ridge of first ch *(Fig. 4, page 45)* to form a ring.

Rnd 1 (Right side)**:** Ch 3 **(counts as first dc)**, dc in back ridge of next ch and each ch around; join with slip st to first dc: 72 dc.

Note: Loop a short piece of yarn around any stitch to mark Rnd 1 as **right** side.

Rnd 2: Ch 2 **(counts as first hdc, now and throughout)**, work FPdc around next dc, ★ work BPdc around next dc, work FPdc around next dc; repeat from ★ around; join with slip st to first hdc.

Rnds 3 and 4: Ch 2, work FPdc around next FPdc, ★ work BPdc around next BPdc, work FPdc around next FPdc; repeat from ★ around; join with slip st to first hdc, finish off.

BODY

Only two colors are used per round. Change colors *(Figs. 2a-d, pages 4 and 5)* carrying the unused color **loosely** on the **back** of the Hat and working over the floats on subsequent rounds *(Figs. 3a & b, page 5)*. Yarn can be carried vertically for 2 rounds. Cut yarns when they are no longer needed.

Work in Back Loops Only *(Fig. 5, page 45)* throughout Body and Crown.

Rnd 1: With **right** side facing, join Color B with sc in same st as joining *(see Joining With Sc, page 45)*; sc in each st around; join with slip st to first sc: 72 sc.

Rnd 2: Ch 1, sc in same st as joining and in each sc around; with Color C, join with slip st to first sc.

Rnd 3: Begin following Hat Chart on page 11 *(see How to Follow a Chart, page 5)*. Ch 1, sc in same st as joining and in next 2 sc changing to Color B in last sc made, ★ sc in next 3 sc changing to Color C in last sc made, sc in next 3 sc changing to Color B in last sc made; repeat from ★ around to last 3 sc, sc in next 3 sc; join with slip st to first sc.

Rnds 4-22: Follow Chart Rnds 4-22.

Rnd 23: Ch 1, sc in same st as joining and in each sc around; with Color B, join with slip st to first sc.

CROWN

Rnd 1: Ch 1, beginning in same st as joining, (sc2tog, sc in next 7 sc) around; join with slip st to first sc: 64 sc.

Rnd 2: Ch 1, beginning in same st as joining, (sc2tog, sc in next 6 sc) around; with Color A, join with slip st to first sc: 56 sc.

Rnd 3: Ch 1, beginning in same st as joining, (sc2tog, sc in next 5 sc) around; join with slip st to first sc: 48 sc.

Rnd 4: Ch 1, beginning in same st as joining, (sc2tog, sc in next 4 sc) around; with Color B, join with slip st to first sc: 40 sc.

Rnd 5: Ch 1, beginning in same st as joining, (sc2tog, sc in next 3 sc) around; join with slip st to first sc: 32 sc.

Rnd 6: Ch 1, beginning in same st as joining, (sc2tog, sc in next 2 sc) around; with Color A, join with slip st to first sc: 24 sc.

Rnd 7: Ch 1, beginning in same st as joining, (sc2tog, sc in next sc) around; join with slip st to first sc: 16 sc.

Rnd 8: Ch 1, beginning in same st as joining, sc2tog around; join with slip st to first sc, finish off leaving a long end for sewing: 8 sc.

Thread yarn needle with long end and weave needle through sc on Rnd 8 ***(Fig. 8, page 46)***; gather tightly to close and secure end.

With all 4 colors, make a 2¾" (7 cm) pom-pom ***(Figs. 10a-c, page 46)***.
Attach pom-pom to top of Hat.

SCARF

Each row is worked across the length of the Scarf.

Always leave a 5" (12.5 cm) end at the beginning and end of each row for fringe.

Only two colors are used per row. Change colors ***(Fig. 2a, page 4)*** carrying the unused color **loosely** on the **back** of the Scarf and working over the floats on subsequent rows ***(Figs. 3a & b, page 5)***.

With Color A and leaving a 5" (12.5 cm) end at beginning, ch 204; finish off leaving a 5" (12.5 cm) end.

Each row is a **right** side row and is worked in Back Loops Only ***(Fig. 5, page 45)*** throughout.

Row 1 (Right side)**:** Working in back ridge of chs ***(Fig. 4, page 45)***, join Color A with sc in first ch ***(see Joining With Sc, page 45)***; sc in each ch across; finish off.

Note: Loop a short piece of yarn around any stitch to mark Row 1 as **right** side.

Row 2: Join Color A with sc in first sc; sc in each sc across; finish off.

Row 3: Begin following Scarf Chart on page 11 ***(see How to Follow a Chart, page 5)***. Join Color A with sc in first sc; sc in next 2 sc changing to Color D in last sc made, ★ sc in next 3 sc changing to Color A in last sc made, sc in next 3 sc changing to Color D in last sc made; repeat from ★ across to last 3 sc, sc in next 3 sc; finish off.

Rows 4-22: Follow Chart Rows 4-22.

FRINGE

Tie groups of 2 ends together in an overhand knot close to Scarf edge to form fringe. Lay flat on a hard surface and trim the ends.

HUGS & KISSES

HAT & COWL

Keep your noggin and neck warm on a chilly fall day. Everyone needs a hug and kiss now and then. The motifs of this set will capture the love.

HUGS & KISSES

HAT & COWL ●●○○ EASY +

SHOPPING LIST

Yarn (Medium Weight) MEDIUM 4

[5 ounces, 256 yards
(141 grams, 234 meters) per skein]:

Hat

- ☐ Color A (Green) - 1 skein
- ☐ Color B (Brown) - 1 skein
- ☐ Color C (Gold) - 1 skein
- ☐ Color D (Dark Green) - 1 skein

Cowl

- ☐ Color A (Green) - 1 skein
- ☐ Color B (Brown) - 1 skein
- ☐ Color C (Gold) - 1 skein
- ☐ Color D (Dark Green) - 1 skein

Crochet Hook

- ☐ Size H (5 mm)
  or size needed for gauge

Additional Supplies

- ☐ Yarn needle (for Hat only)

GAUGE INFORMATION

In Fair Isle pattern,
15 sc and 15 rows/rnds = 4" (10 cm)

Gauge Swatch: 4" (10 cm) square

Ch 15; finish off.

Row 1 (Right side)**:** Working in back ridge of chs ***(Fig. 4, page 45)***, join yarn with sc in first ch ***(see Joining With Sc, page 45)***; sc in each ch across; finish off: 15 sc.

Rows 2-15: With **right** side facing and working in Back Loops Only ***(Fig. 5, page 45)***, join yarn with sc in first sc; sc in each sc across; finish off.

FINISHED SIZES **Hat:** Finished circumference 19¼" (49 cm)

Cowl: 5" high x 21¼" circumference (12.5 cm x 54 cm)

STITCH GUIDE

FRONT POST DOUBLE CROCHET
(abbreviated FPdc)
YO, insert hook from **front** to **back** around post of st indicated ***(Fig. 7, page 46)***, YO and pull up a loop (3 loops on hook), (YO and draw through 2 loops on hook) twice.

BACK POST DOUBLE CROCHET
(abbreviated BPdc)
YO, insert hook from **back** to **front** around post of st indicated ***(Fig. 7, page 46)***, YO and pull up a loop (3 loops on hook), (YO and draw through 2 loops on hook) twice.

SINGLE CROCHET 2 TOGETHER
(abbreviated sc2tog)
Pull up a loop in each of next 2 sc, YO and draw through all 3 loops on hook **(counts as one sc)**.

HAT CHART

Write the color name of the yarn you're using in the Color Key.

COLOR KEY

- Color A ________

- Color B ________

- Color C ________

- Color D ________

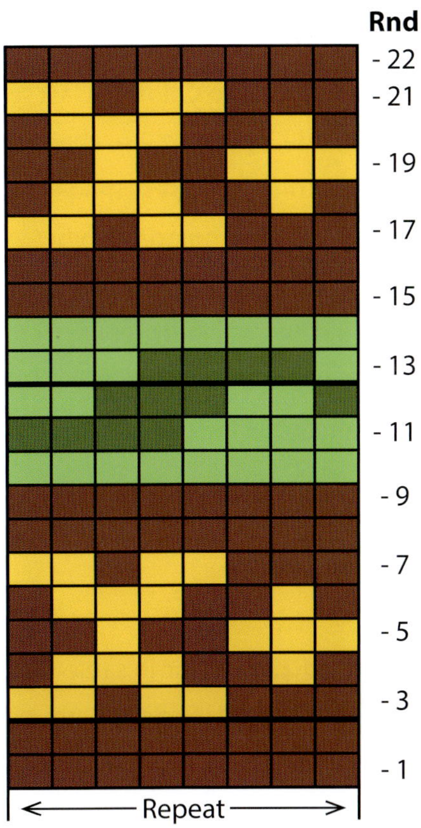

On all rounds, follow the Chart from **right** to **left.**

COWL CHART

Write the color name of the yarn you're using in the Color Key.

COLOR KEY

- Color A ________

- Color B ________

- Color C ________

- Color D ________

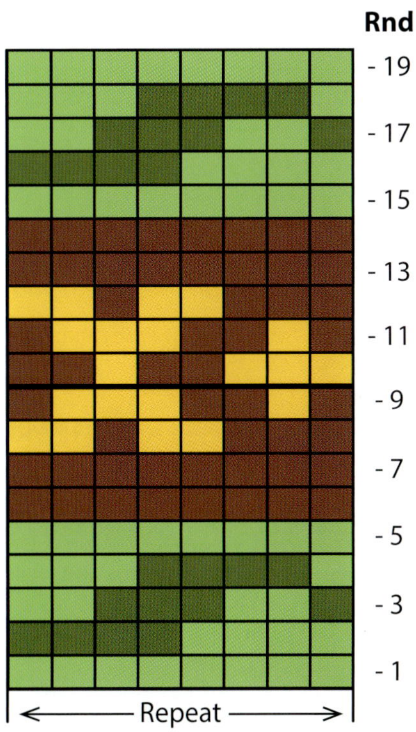

On all rounds, follow the Chart from **right** to **left.**

HAT

RIBBING

With Color A, ch 72; being careful **not** to twist ch, join with slip st to back ridge of first ch ***(Fig. 4, page 45)*** to form a ring.

Rnd 1 (Right side)**:** Ch 3 **(counts as first dc)**, dc in back ridge of next ch and each ch around; join with slip st to first dc: 72 dc.

Note: Loop a short piece of yarn around any stitch to mark Rnd 1 as **right** side.

Rnd 2: Ch 2 **(counts as first hdc, now and throughout)**, work FPdc around next dc, ★ work BPdc around next dc, work FPdc around next dc; repeat from ★ around; join with slip st to first hdc.

Rnds 3 and 4: Ch 2, work FPdc around next FPdc, ★ work BPdc around next BPdc, work FPdc around next FPdc; repeat from ★ around; join with slip st to first hdc, finish off.

BODY

Only two colors are used per round. Change colors ***(Figs. 2a-d, pages 4 and 5)*** carrying the unused color **loosely** on the **back** of the Hat and working over the floats on subsequent rounds ***(Figs. 3a & b, page 5)***. Yarn can be carried vertically for 2 rounds. Cut yarns when they are no longer needed.

Work in Back Loops Only ***(Fig. 5, page 45)*** throughout Body and Crown.

Rnd 1: With **right** side facing, join Color B with sc in same st as joining ***(see Joining With Sc, page 45)***; sc in each st around; join with slip st to first sc: 72 sc.

Rnd 2: Ch 1, sc in same st as joining and in each sc around; join with slip st to first sc.

Rnd 3: Begin following Hat Chart on page 21 ***(see How to Follow a Chart, page 5)***. Ch 1, sc in same st as joining and in next 2 sc changing to Color C in last sc made, sc in next 2 sc changing to Color B in last sc made, sc in next sc changing to Color C, sc in next 2 sc changing to Color B in last sc made, ★ sc in next 3 sc changing to Color C in last sc made, sc in next 2 sc changing to Color B in last sc made, sc in next sc changing to Color C, sc in next 2 sc changing to Color B in last sc made; repeat from ★ around; join with slip st to first sc.

Rnd 4-22: Follow Chart Rnds 4-22.

Rnd 23: Ch 1, sc in same st as joining and in each sc around; with Color A, join with slip st to first sc.

CROWN

Rnd 1: Ch 1, beginning in same st as joining, (sc2tog, sc in next 7 sc) around; join with slip st to first sc: 64 sc.

Rnd 2: Ch 1, beginning in same st as joining, (sc2tog, sc in next 6 sc) around; join with slip st to first sc: 56 sc.

Rnd 3: Ch 1, beginning in same st as joining, (sc2tog, sc in next 5 sc) around; join with slip st to first sc: 48 sc.

Rnd 4: Ch 1, beginning in same st as joining, (sc2tog, sc in next 4 sc) around; join with slip st to first sc: 40 sc.

Rnd 5: Ch 1, beginning in same st as joining, (sc2tog, sc in next 3 sc) around; join with slip st to first sc: 32 sc.

Rnd 6: Ch 1, beginning in same st as joining, (sc2tog, sc in next 2 sc) around; join with slip st to first sc: 24 sc.

Rnd 7: Ch 1, beginning in same st as joining, (sc2tog, sc in next sc) around; join with slip st to first sc: 16 sc.

Rnd 8: Ch 1, beginning in same st as joining, sc2tog around; join with slip st to first sc, finish off leaving a long end for sewing: 8 sc.

Thread yarn needle with long end and weave needle through sc on Rnd 8 ***(Fig. 8, page 46)***; gather tightly to close and secure end.

COWL

With Color A, ch 80; being careful not to twist ch, join with slip st to back ridge of first ch ***(Fig. 4, page 45)*** to form a ring.

Rnd 1 (Right side)**:** Ch 1, sc in same ch and in back ridge of each ch around: 80 sc.

Note: Loop a short piece of yarn around any stitch to mark Rnd 1 as **right** side.

Only two colors are used per round. Change colors ***(Figs. 2a & b, pages 4 and 5)*** carrying the unused color **loosely** on the **back** of the Cowl and working over the floats on subsequent rounds ***(Figs. 3a & b, page 5)***. Yarn can be carried vertically for 2 rounds. Cut yarns when they are no longer needed.

Work in Back Loops Only ***(Fig. 5, page 45)*** throughout.

Rnd 2: Begin following Cowl Chart on page 21 ***(see How to Follow a Chart, page 5)***. Ch 1, sc in same st as joining and in next 3 sc changing to Color D in last sc made, ★ sc in next 4 sc changing to Color A in last sc made, sc in next 4 sc changing to Color D in last sc made; repeat from ★ around to last 4 sc, sc in last 4 sc; join with slip st to first sc.

Rnds 3-19: Follow Chart Rnds 3-19.

Finish off.

STARS & DIAMONDS

AFGHAN & PILLOW

Cozy up with a stars and diamonds duo at the campsite. Sitting around the fire and toasting marshmallows just got comfy.

STARS & DIAMONDS

AFGHAN & PILLOW ●●○○ EASY +

•△

SHOPPING LIST

Yarn (Medium Weight) MEDIUM 4

[6 ounces, 315 yards
(170 grams, 288 meters) per skein]:

Afghan

- ☐ Main Color (Green) - 4 skeins
- ☐ Contrasting Color (Off White) - 4 skeins

Pillow

- ☐ Main Color (Green) - 1 skein
- ☐ Contrasting Color (Off White) - 1 skein

Crochet Hook

Afghan

- ☐ Size G (4 mm) **or** size needed for gauge

Pillow

- ☐ Size I (5.5 mm) **or** size needed for gauge

Additional Supplies

For Pillow Only

- ☐ Fabric - 1¼ yards (1.15 meters)
- ☐ Polyester fiberfill
- ☐ 1¼" (32 mm) Buttons - 4
- ☐ Sewing needle and matching thread

•△

FINISHED SIZES **Afghan:** 43" x 47½" (109 cm x 120.5 cm)
Pillow: 15½" wide x 18½" long (39.5 cm x 47 cm)

GAUGE INFORMATION

Afghan

With smaller size hook, in Fair Isle pattern,
16 sc and 13 rows = 4" (10 cm)

Gauge Swatch: 4" (10 cm) square

With smaller size hook, ch 16; finish off.

Row 1 (Right side)**:** Working in back ridge of chs ***(Fig. 4, page 45)***, join yarn with sc in first ch ***(see Joining With Sc, page 45)***; sc in each ch across; finish off: 15 sc.

Rows 2-13: With **right** side facing and working in Back Loops Only ***(Fig. 5, page 45)***, join yarn with sc in first sc; sc in each sc across; finish off.

Pillow

With larger size hook, in Fair Isle pattern,
14 sc and 12 rnds/rows = 4" (10 cm)

Gauge Swatch: 4" (10 cm) square

With larger size hook, ch 14; finish off.

Row 1 (Right side)**:** Working in back ridge of chs ***(Fig. 4, page 45)***, join yarn with sc in first ch ***(see Joining With Sc, page 45)***; sc in each ch across; finish off: 14 sc.

Rows 2-12: With **right** side facing and working in Back Loops Only ***(Fig. 5, page 45)***, join yarn with sc in first sc; sc in each sc across; finish off.

CHART

Write the color name of the yarn you're using in the Color Key.

COLOR KEY

- Main Color ________

- Contrasting Color ________

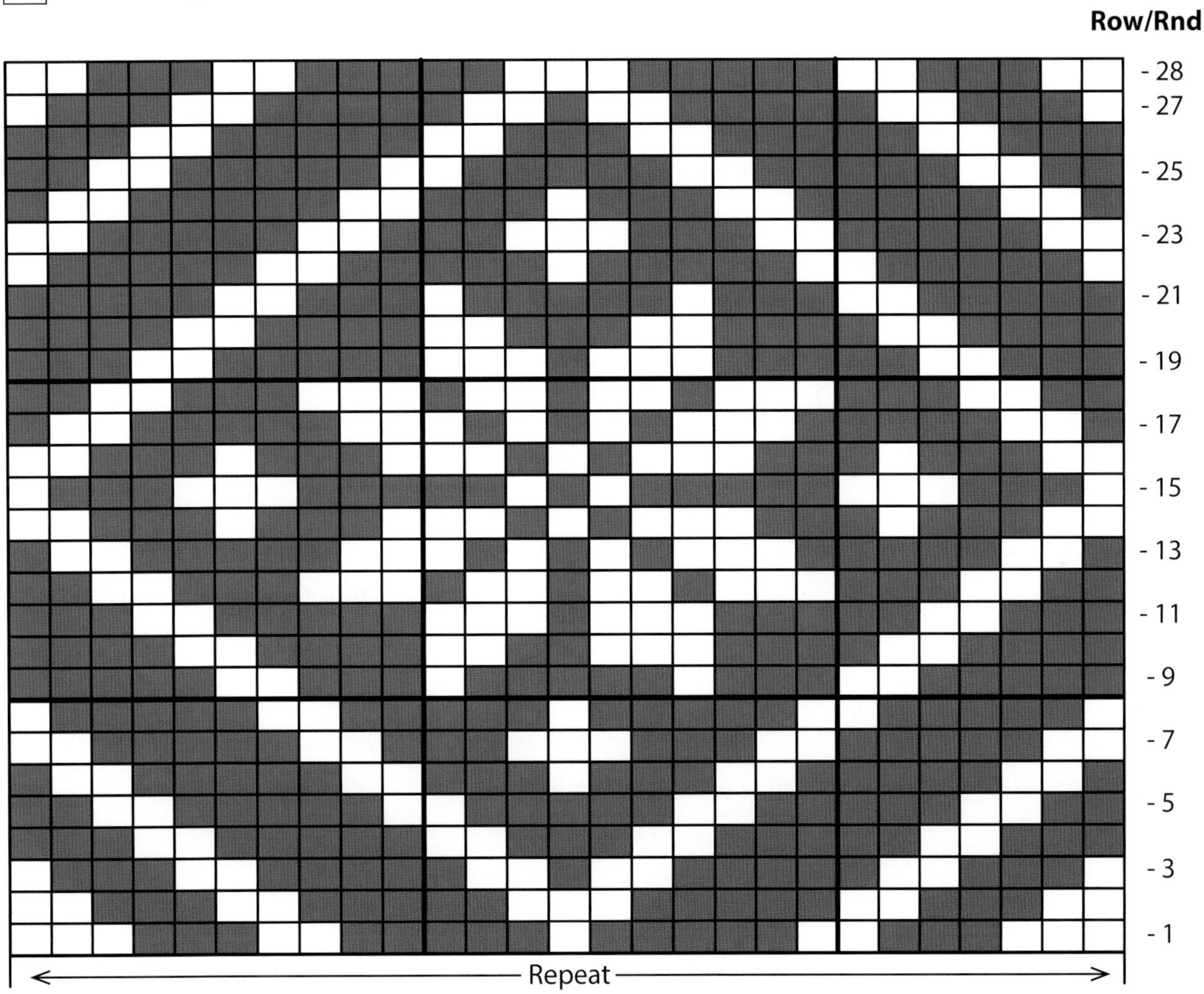

On all rows/rounds, follow the Chart from **right** to **left.**

AFGHAN

Each row is a **right** side row worked across the length of the Afghan and in Back Loops Only *(Fig. 5, page 45)* throughout.

Always leave a 6" (15 cm) end of both colors at beginning and end of each row for fringe. When working rows with 2 colors, begin and end each row by working the first color over the second color.

Change colors *(Fig. 2a, page 4)* carrying the unused color **loosely** on the **back** of the Afghan and working over the floats on subsequent rows *(Figs. 3a & b, page 5)*.

BODY

∆•∆•∆•∆•

With Contrasting Color and leaving a 6" (15 cm) end at beginning, ch 189; finish off leaving a 6" (15 cm) end.

Foundation Row (Right side)**:** Working over a second strand of Contrasting Color and in back ridge of chs *(Fig. 4, page 45)*, join Contrasting Color with sc in first ch *(see Joining With Sc, page 45)*; sc in each ch across; finish off.

Note: Loop a short piece of yarn around any stitch to mark Foundation Row as **right** side.

Row 1: Begin following Afghan Chart on page 29 *(see How to Follow a Chart, page 5)*. Join Contrasting Color with sc in first sc; sc in next 2 sc changing to Main Color in last sc made, sc in next 3 sc changing to Contrasting Color in last sc made, sc in next 2 sc changing to Main Color in last sc made, sc in next 5 sc changing to Contrasting Color in last sc made, sc in next sc changing to Main Color, sc in next 5 sc changing to Contrasting Color in last sc made, sc in next 2 sc changing to Main Color in last sc made, sc in next 3 sc changing to Contrasting Color in last sc made, sc in next 3 sc, ★ sc in next 3 sc changing to Main Color in last sc made, sc in next 3 sc changing to Contrasting Color in last sc made, sc in next 2 sc changing to Main Color in last sc made, sc in next 5 sc changing to Contrasting Color in last sc made, sc in next sc changing to Main Color, sc in next 5 sc changing to Contrasting Color in last sc made, sc in next 2 sc changing to Main Color in last sc made, sc in next 3 sc changing to Contrasting Color in last sc made, sc in next 3 sc; repeat from ★ across; finish off.

Rows 2-139: Follow Chart Rows 2-28 once; then repeat Rows 1-28, 4 times.

Row 140: Working over a second strand of Contrasting Color, join Contrasting Color with sc in first sc; sc in each sc across; finish off.

FRINGE

∆•∆•∆•∆•∆

Tie groups of approximately 4 ends together in an overhand knot close to Afghan edge to form fringe. Lay flat on a hard surface and trim the ends.

PILLOW

Each round is a **right** side round and is worked in Back Loops Only *(Fig. 5, page 45)* throughout.

Change colors *(Figs. 2a-d, pages 4 and 5)* carrying the unused color loosely on the **wrong** side of the Pillow and working over the floats on subsequent rounds *(Figs. 3a & b, page 5)*. Yarn can be carried vertically for 2 rounds. Cut yarns when they are no longer needed.

BODY

With Main Color, ch 108; being careful not to twist ch, join with slip st to back ridge of first ch *(Fig. 4, page 45)* to form a ring.

Foundation Rnd (Right side)**:** Ch 1, sc in back ridge of same ch as joining and each ch around; with Contrasting Color join with slip st to first sc: 108 sc.

Note: Loop a short piece of yarn around any stitch to mark Foundation Rnd as **right** side.

Rnd 1: Begin following Pillow Chart on page 29 *(see How to Follow a Chart, page 5)*. Ch 1, sc in same st as joining and in next 2 sc changing to Main Color in last sc made, sc in next 3 sc changing to Contrasting Color in last sc made, sc in next 2 sc changing to Main Color in last sc made, sc in next 5 sc changing to Contrasting Color in last sc made, sc in next sc changing to Main Color, sc in next 5 sc changing to Contrasting Color in last sc made, sc in next 2 sc changing to Main Color in last sc made, sc in next 3 sc changing to Contrasting Color in last sc made, sc in next 3 sc, ★ sc in next 3 sc changing to Main Color in last sc made, sc in next 3 sc changing to Contrasting Color in last sc made, sc in next 2 sc changing to Main Color in last sc made, sc in next 5 sc changing to Contrasting Color in last sc made, sc in next sc changing to Main Color, sc in next 5 sc changing to Contrasting Color in last sc made, sc in next 2 sc changing to Main Color in last sc in last sc made, sc in next 3 sc changing to Contrasting Color in last sc made, sc in next 3 sc; repeat from ★ around; join with slip st to first sc.

Rnds 2-56: Follow Chart Rows 2-28 once; then repeat Rnds 1-28 once; at end of Rnd 56, change to Main Color.

BUTTONHOLE BAND

Row 1: Ch 1, do **not** turn; sc in Back Loop Only of same st as joining and next 53 sc, leave remaining 54 sc unworked.

Rows 2 and 3: Ch 1, **turn**; sc in both loops of each sc across.

Row 4: Ch 1, turn; sc in first 8 sc, ★ ch 3, skip next 3 sc, sc in next 9 sc, ch 3, skip next 3 sc, sc in next 8 sc; repeat from ★ once **more**: 42 sc and 4 ch-3 sps (4 buttonholes).

Row 5: Ch 1, turn; sc in first 8 sc, ★ 3 sc in next ch-3 sp, sc in next 9 sc, 3 sc in next ch-3 sp, sc in next 8 sc; repeat from ★ once **more**: 54 sc.

Row 6: Ch 1, turn; sc in each sc across; finish off.

PILLOW FORM

Using flattened Body as a pattern, excluding the Buttonhole Band, cut fabric adding a ½" (12 mm) seam allowance on each side. With **right** sides together, sew seam, leaving a 2" (5 cm) opening for turning.

Clip corners and turn right side out. Stuff firmly with polyester fiberfill and sew opening closed.

FLANGE

Rnd 1: With **right** side facing, working in free loops of sc on Rnd 56 ***(Fig. 6a, page 45)***, join Main Color with slip st in first sc in front of Buttonhole Band; ch 2 **(counts as first hdc, now and throughout)**, 2 hdc in same st, hdc in next 52 sc, 5 hdc in last sc; working through **both** layers (at fold), hdc in each rnd across; working in free loops of beginning ch and through **both** layers ***(Fig. 6b, page 45)***, 5 hdc in first ch, hdc in each ch across to last ch, 5 hdc in last ch; working through **both** layers (at fold), hdc in each rnd across; 2 hdc in same st as first hdc; join with slip st to first hdc: 236 hdc.

Rnds 2-7: Ch 2, 2 hdc in same st as joining, ★ hdc in each hdc across to center hdc of next corner 5-hdc group, 5 hdc in center hdc; repeat from ★ 2 times **more**, hdc in each hdc across, 2 hdc in same st as first hdc; join with slip st to first hdc.

Finish off.

Sew buttons to Body opposite buttonholes.

Insert pillow form.

ZIGZAGS & DIAMONDS

AFGHAN & PILLOW

Capture the blues and clouds of an autumn afternoon sky. And when night does fall, you will be well-prepared for the chill with this afghan and pillow set.

ZIGZAGS & DIAMONDS

AFGHAN & PILLOW ●●○○ EASY +

SHOPPING LIST

Yarn (Medium Weight) MEDIUM 4

[6 ounces, 315 yards

(170 grams, 288 meters) per skein]:

Afghan

- ☐ Color A (Off White) - 4 skeins
- ☐ Color B (Dark Blue) - 4 skeins
- ☐ Color C (Blue) - 2 skeins
- ☐ Color D (Light Blue) - 2 skeins

Pillow

- ☐ Color A (Off White) - 1 skein
- ☐ Color B (Dark Blue) - 1 skein
- ☐ Color C (Blue) - 1 skein
- ☐ Color D (Light Blue) - 1 skein

Crochet Hook

Afghan

- ☐ Size G (4 mm)
  or size needed for gauge

Pillow

- ☐ Size H (5 mm)
  or size needed for gauge

Additional Supplies

For Pillow Only

- ☐ Fabric - 1¼ yards (1.15 meters)
- ☐ Polyester fiberfill
- ☐ 1¼" (32 mm) Buttons - 4
- ☐ Sewing needle and matching thread
- ☐ Yarn needle

FINISHED SIZES

Afghan: 42" x 46½" (106.5 cm x 118 cm)

Pillow: 15" wide x 20½" long (38 cm x 52 cm)

GAUGE INFORMATION

Afghan

With larger size hook, in Fair Isle pattern,
15 sc and 14 rows = 4" (10 cm)

Gauge Swatch: 4" (10 cm) square

With larger size hook, ch 15; finish off.

Row 1 (Right side)**:** Working in back ridge of chs ***(Fig. 4, page 45)***, join yarn with sc in first ch ***(see Joining With Sc, page 45)***; sc in each ch across; finish off: 15 sc.

Rows 2-14: With **right** side facing and working in Back Loops Only ***(Fig. 5, page 45)***, join yarn with sc in first sc; sc in each sc across; finish off.

Pillow

With smaller size hook, in Fair Isle pattern,
16 sc and 13 rows/rnds = 4" (10 cm)

Gauge Swatch: 4" (10 cm) square

With smaller size hook, ch 16; finish off.

Row 1 (Right side)**:** Working in back ridge of chs ***(Fig. 4, page 45)***, join yarn with sc in first ch ***(see Joining With Sc, page 45)***; sc in each ch across; finish off: 15 sc.

Rows 2-13: With **right** side facing and working in Back Loops Only ***(Fig. 5, page 45)***, join yarn with sc in first sc; sc in each sc across; finish off.

AFGHAN CHART

Write the color name of the yarn you're using in the Color Key.

COLOR KEY

- Color A ________
- Color B ________
- Color C ________
- Color D ________

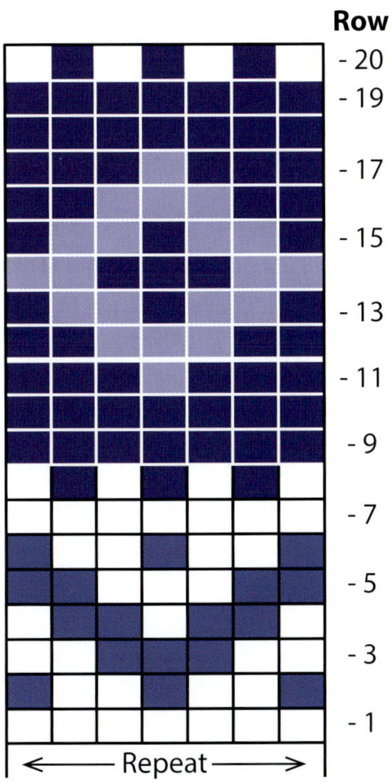

On all rows, follow the Chart from **right** to **left.**

PILLOW CHART

Write the color name of the yarn you're using in the Color Key.

COLOR KEY

- Color A ________
- Color B ________
- Color C ________
- Color D ________

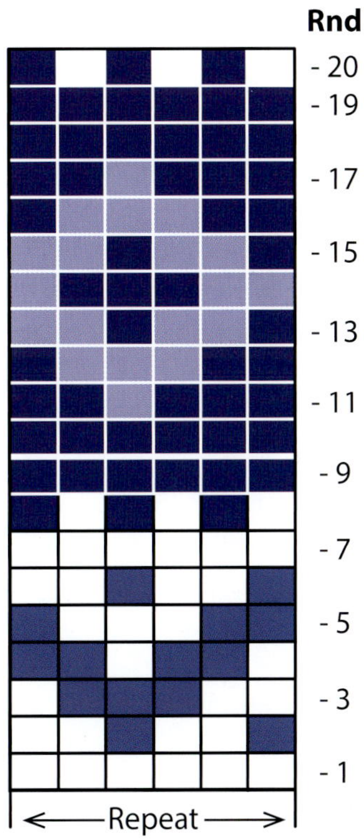

On all rounds, follow the Chart from **right** to **left.**

AFGHAN

Each row is a **right** side row, worked across the length of the Afghan and in Back Loops Only ***(Fig. 5, page 45)*** throughout.

Always leave a 6" (15 cm) end of both colors at beginning and end of each row for fringe.

When working rows with 2 colors, begin and end each row by working the first color over the second color. When working rows with one color, work over a second strand of the same color.

Change colors ***(Fig. 2a, page 4)*** carrying the unused color loosely on the back of the Afghan and working over the floats on subsequent rows ***(Figs. 3a & b, page 5)***.

BODY

With Color A and leaving a 6" (15 cm) end at beginning, ch 175; finish off leaving a 6" (15 cm) end.

Row 1 (Right side)**:** Working in back ridge of chs ***(Fig. 4, page 45)***, join Color A with sc in first ch ***(see Joining With Sc, page 45)***; sc in each ch across; finish off.

Note: Loop a short piece of yarn around any stitch to mark Row 1 as **right** side.

Row 2: Begin following Afghan Chart on page 39 ***(see How to Follow a Chart, page 5)***. Join Color C with sc in first sc changing to Color A; sc in next 2 sc changing to Color C in last sc made, sc in next sc changing to Color A, sc in next 2 sc changing to Color C in last sc made, ★ sc in next sc changing to Color A, sc in next 2 sc changing to Color C in last sc made, sc in next sc changing to Color A, sc in next 2 sc; repeat from ★ across to last sc, sc in last sc; finish off.

Rows 3-147: Follow Chart Rows 3-20 once; then repeat Rows 1-20, 6 times; then repeat Rows 1-7 once **more**.

FRINGE

Tie groups of approximately 4 ends together in an overhand knot close to Afghan edge to form fringe. Lay flat on a hard surface and trim the ends.

PILLOW

Change colors ***(Figs. 2a-d, pages 4 and 5)*** carrying the unused color loosely on the **wrong** side of the Pillow and working over the floats on subsequent rounds ***(Figs. 3a & b, page 5)***. Yarn can be carried vertically for 2 rounds. Cut yarns when they are no longer needed.

Each round is a **right** side round and is worked in Back Loops Only ***(Fig. 5, page 45)*** throughout.

BODY

With Color A, ch 120; being careful not to twist ch, join with slip st to back ridge of first ch ***(Fig. 4, page 45)*** to form a ring.

Rnd 1 (Right side)**:** Ch 1, sc in back ridge of same ch as joining and each ch around; with Color C, join with slip st to first sc: 120 sc.

Note: Loop a short piece of yarn around any stitch to mark Rnd 1 as **right** side.

Rnd 2: Begin following Pillow Chart on page 39 ***(see How to Follow a Chart, page 5)***. Ch 1, sc in same st as joining changing to Color A, sc in next 2 sc changing to Color C in last sc made, sc in next sc changing to Color A, sc in next 2 sc changing to Color C in last sc made, ★ sc in next sc changing to Color A, sc in next 2 sc changing to Color C in last sc made, sc in next sc changing to Color A, sc in next 2 sc; repeat from ★ around; join with slip st to first sc.

Rnds 3-67: Following Chart for color changes, Rnds 3-20 once; then repeat Rnds 1-20 twice; then repeat Rnds 1-7 once **more**; at the end of Rnd 67, do **not** finish off Off White.

BUTTONHOLE BAND

Row 1: Ch 1, do **not** turn; sc in Back Loop Only of same st as joining and next 59 sc, leave remaining 60 sc unworked.

Rows 2 and 3: Ch 1, **turn**; sc in both loops of each sc across.

Row 4: Ch 1, turn; sc in first 3 sc, ch 3, skip next 3 sc, ★ sc in next 14 sc, ch 3, skip next 3 sc; repeat from ★ 2 times **more**, sc in last 3 sc: 48 sc and 4 ch-3 sps (4 buttonholes).

Row 5: Ch 1, turn; sc in first 3 sc, 3 sc in next ch-3 sp, (sc in next 14 sc, 3 sc in next ch-3 sp) 3 times, sc in last sc: 60 sc.

Row 6: Ch 1, turn; sc in each sc across; finish off.

PILLOW FORM

Using flattened Body as a pattern, excluding the Buttonhole Band, cut fabric adding a ½" (12 mm) seam allowance on each side. With **right** sides together, sew seam, leaving a 2" (5 cm) opening for turning.

Clip corners and turn right side out. Stuff firmly with polyester fiberfill and sew opening closed.

Flatten Body, working in free loops of beginning ch and through **both** layers ***(Fig. 6b, page 45)***, whipstitch bottom seam ***(Fig. 9, page 46)***.

Sew buttons to Body opposite buttonholes.

Insert pillow form.

General Instructions

ABBREVIATIONS

BPdc	Back Post double crochet
ch(s)	chain(s)
cm	centimeters
dc	double crochet(s)
FPdc	Front Post double crochet
hdc	half double crochet(s)
mm	millimeters
Rnd(s)	Round(s)
sc	single crochet(s)
sc2tog	single crochet 2 together
sp(s)	space(s)
st(s)	stitch(es)
YO	yarn over

SYMBOLS & TERMS

★ — work instructions following ★ as many **more** times as indicated in addition to the first time.

( ) or **[ ]** — work enclosed instructions **as many** times as specified by the number immediately following **or** contains explanatory remarks.

colon (:) — the number(s) given after a colon at the end of a row or round denote(s) the number of stitches or spaces you should have on that row or round.

CROCHET TERMINOLOGY		
UNITED STATES		INTERNATIONAL
slip stitch (slip st)	=	single crochet (sc)
single crochet (sc)	=	double crochet (dc)
half double crochet (hdc)	=	half treble crochet (htr)
double crochet (dc)	=	treble crochet (tr)
treble crochet (tr)	=	double treble crochet (dtr)
double treble crochet (dtr)	=	triple treble crochet (ttr)
triple treble crochet (tr tr)	=	quadruple treble crochet (qtr)
skip	=	miss

Yarn Weight Symbol & Names	LACE 0	SUPER FINE 1	FINE 2	LIGHT 3	MEDIUM 4	BULKY 5	SUPER BULKY 6	JUMBO 7
Type of Yarns in Category	Fingering, size 10 crochet thread	Sock, Fingering, Baby	Sport, Baby	DK, Light Worsted	Worsted, Afghan, Aran	Chunky, Craft, Rug	Super Bulky, Roving	Jumbo, Roving
Crochet Gauge* Ranges in Single Crochet to 4" (10 cm)	32-42 sts**	21-32 sts	16-20 sts	12-17 sts	11-14 sts	8-11 sts	6-9 sts	5 sts and fewer
Advised Hook Size Range	Steel*** 6 to 8, Regular hook B-1	B-1 to E-4	E-4 to 7	7 to I-9	I-9 to K-10½	K-10½ to M/N-13	M/N-13 to Q	Q and larger

*GUIDELINES ONLY: The chart above reflects the most commonly used gauges and hook sizes for specific yarn categories.

** Lace weight yarns are usually crocheted with larger hooks to create lacy openwork patterns. Accordingly, a gauge range is difficult to determine. Always follow the gauge stated in your pattern.

*** Steel crochet hooks are sized differently from regular hooks–the higher the number, the smaller the hook, which is the reverse of regular hook sizing.

GAUGE

Exact gauge is **essential** for proper size. Before beginning your project, make the sample swatch given in the individual instructions in the yarn and hook specified. After completing the swatch, measure it, counting your stitches and rows carefully. If your swatch is larger or smaller than specified, **make another, changing hook size to get the correct gauge**. Keep trying until you find the size hook that will give you the specified gauge.

JOINING WITH SC

When instructed to join with sc, begin with a slip knot on hook. Insert hook in stitch indicated, YO and pull up a loop, YO and draw through both loops on hook.

BACK RIDGE

Work only in loops indicated by arrows ***(Fig. 4)***.

Fig. 4

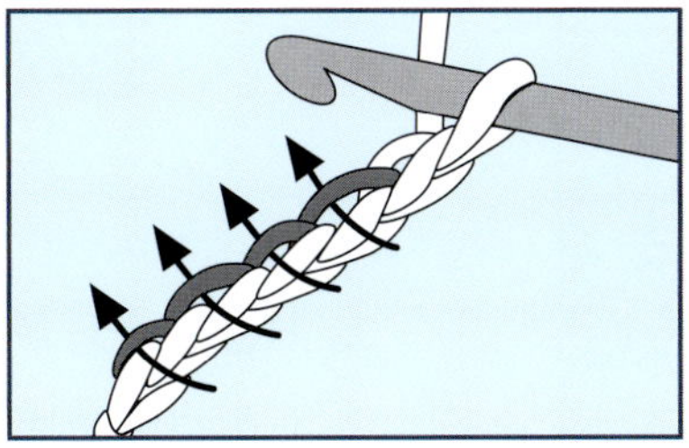

BACK LOOPS ONLY

Work only in loop(s) indicated by arrow ***(Fig. 5)***.

Fig. 5

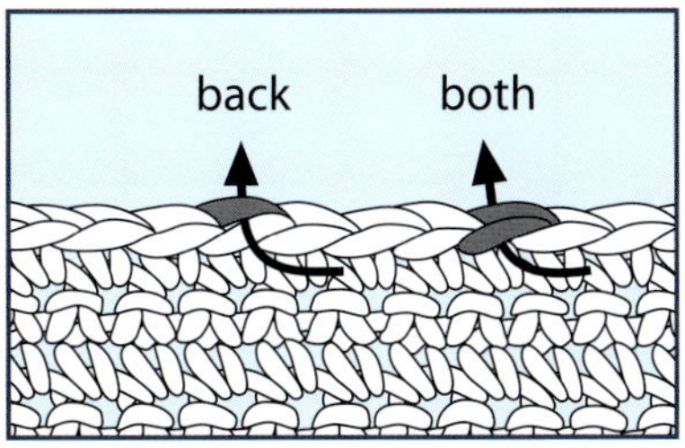

FREE LOOPS

After working in Back Loops Only on a row or round, there will be a ridge of unused loops called the free loops. Later, when instructed to work in the free loops of the same row or round, work in these loops ***(Fig. 6a)***.

When instructed to work in free loops of a chain, work in loop indicated by arrow ***(Fig. 6b)***.

Fig. 6a

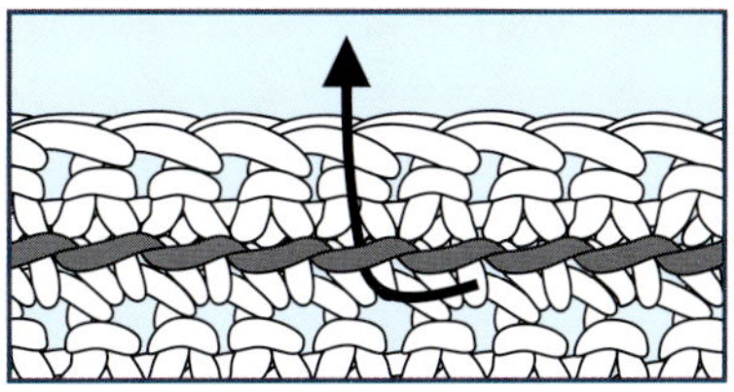

Fig. 6b

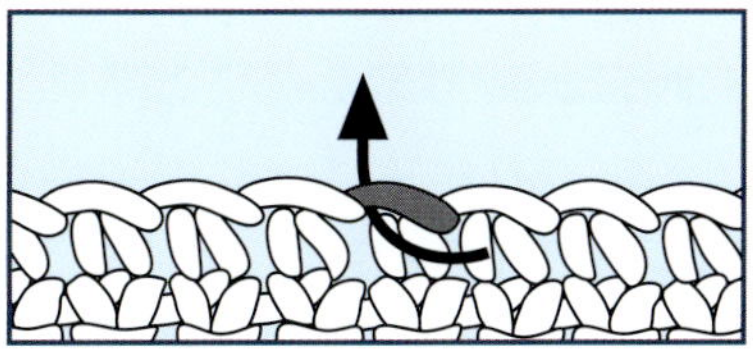

CROCHET HOOKS																	
U.S.	B-1	C-2	D-3	E-4	F-5	G-6	7	H-8	I-9	J-10	K-10½	L-11	M/N-13	N/P-15	P/Q	Q	S
Metric - mm	2.25	2.75	3.25	3.5	3.75	4	4.5	5	5.5	6	6.5	8	9	10	15	16	19

●○○○ **BEGINNER**	Projects for first-time crocheters using basic stitches. Minimal shaping.
●●○○ **EASY**	Projects using yarn with basic stitches, repetitive stitch patterns, simple color changes, and simple shaping and finishing.
●●●○ **INTERMEDIATE**	Projects using a variety of techniques, such as basic lace patterns or color patterns, mid-level shaping and finishing.
●●●● **EXPERIENCED**	Projects with intricate stitch patterns, techniques and dimension, such as non-repeating patterns, multi-color techniques, fine threads, small hooks, detailed shaping and refined finishing.

POST STITCH

Work around post of stitch indicated, inserting hook in direction of arrow *(Fig. 7)*.

Fig. 7

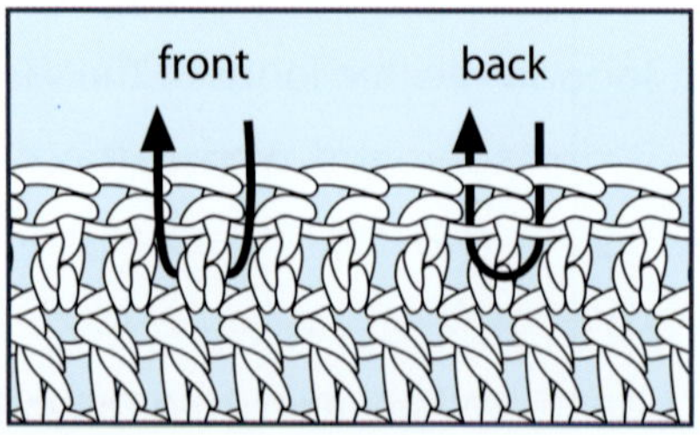

WEAVE THRU STITCHES

Weave yarn end through the stitches *(Fig. 8)* and gather to close.

Fig. 8

WHIPSTITCH

With **wrong** side together, sew through **both** layers once to secure the beginning of the seam, leaving an ample yarn end to weave in later. Working through **both** loops of each stitch on **both** pieces *(Fig. 9)*, insert the needle from **back** to **front** and pull yarn through. ★ Bring the needle around and insert it from **back** to **front** through next stitch and pull yarn through; repeat from ★ across.

Fig. 9

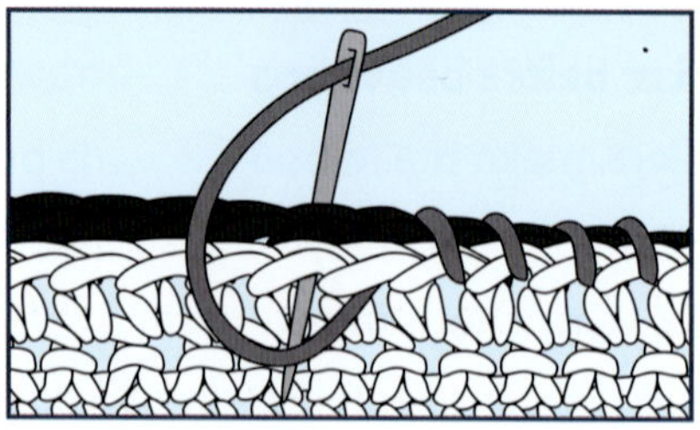

POM-POM

Cut a piece of cardboard 3" (7.5 cm) wide and as long as you want the diameter of your finished pom-pom to be.

Wind the yarn around the cardboard until it is approximately ½" (12 mm) thick in the middle *(Fig. 10a)*. Carefully slip the yarn off the cardboard and firmly tie an 18" (45.5 cm) length of yarn around the middle *(Fig. 10b)*. Leave yarn ends long enough to attach the pom-pom. Cut the loops on both ends and trim the pom-pom into a smooth ball *(Fig. 10c)*.

Fig. 10a

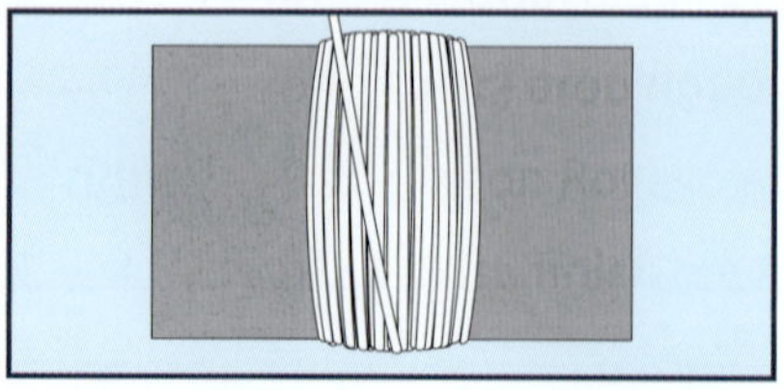

Fig. 10b

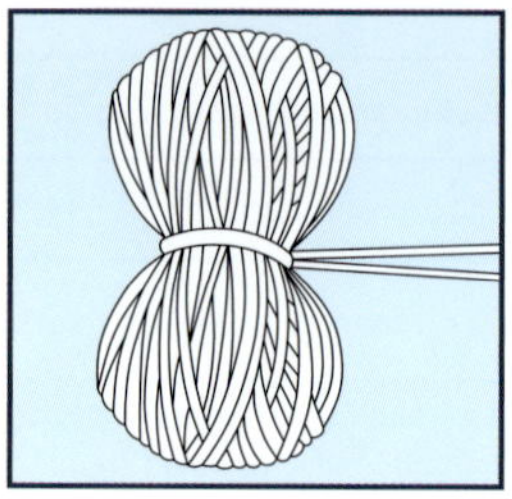

Fig. 10c

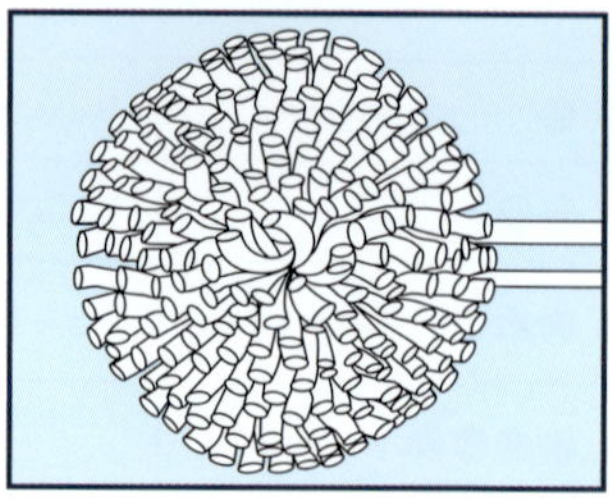

Yarn Information

The projects in this book were made using Medium Weight Yarn. Any brand of Medium Weight Yarn may be used. It is best to refer to the yardage/meters when determining how many balls or skeins to purchase. Remember, to arrive at the finished size, it is the GAUGE/TENSION that is important, not the brand of yarn.

For your convenience, listed below are the specific yarns used to create our photography models. Because yarn manufacturers make frequent changes in their product lines, you may sometimes find it necessary to use a substitute yarn or to search for the discontinued product at alternate suppliers (locally or online).

LAUREL LEAVES HAT & SCARF

Lion Brand® Wool-Ease®

Color A (Black) - #153 Black

Color B (Ecru) - #099 Fisherman

Color C (Red) - #138 Cranberry

Color D (Grey) - #151 Grey Heather

HUGS & KISSES HAT & COWL

Red Heart® Soft®

Color A (Green) - #9522 Leaf

Color B (Brown) - #9344 Chocolate

Color C (Gold) - #9114 Honey

Color D (Dark Green) - #9523 Dark Leaf

STARS & DIAMONDS AFGHAN & PILLOW

Caron® Simply Soft®

Main Color (Green) - #9707 Dark Sage

Contrasting Color (Off White) - #9702 Off White

ZIGZAGS & DIAMONDS AFGHAN & PILLOW

Caron® Simply Soft®

Color A (Off White) - #9702 Off White

Color B (Dark Blue) - #9711 Dark Country Blue

Color C (Blue) - #9784 Cobalt Blue

Color D (Light Blue) - #9709 Light Country Blue

Meet Melissa Leapman

With more than 800 knit and crochet designs in print, Melissa Leapman is one of the most widely published American designers working today.

She began her design career by freelancing for leading ready-to-wear design houses in New York City. She also created designs to help top yarn companies promote their new and existing yarns each season. Her ability to quickly develop fully envisioned garments put her skills in great demand.

Through the years, Leisure Arts has published more than 40 books of Melissa's fabulous designs. Melissa is also the host of several Leisure Arts DVDs in the best-selling teach-yourself series, "I Can't Believe I'm Knitting" and "I Can't Believe I'm Crocheting."

Nationally, her designs have been featured in numerous magazines, and her workshops on knitting and crochet are consistently popular with crafters of all skill levels. She has taught at major events such as STITCHES, Vogue Knitting LIVE, and The Knitting Guild Association conferences, as well as at hundreds of yarn shops and local guild events across the country.

Look for other Leisure Arts books featuring Melissa's designs at www.leisurearts.com/meet-the-designers/melissa-leapman.html.

Production Team: Instructional/Technical Writer - Lois J. Long; Editorial Writer - Susan Frantz Wiles; Senior Graphic Artist - Lora Puls; Graphic Artist - Amy L. Teeter; Photo Stylist - Lori Wenger; and Photographer - Jason Masters.

Made in U.S.A.